ARTIST TRANSCRIPTIONS PIANO

Count Basie COLLECTION

ISBN 0-634-05977-7

HAL•LEONARD®
CORPORATION

7777 W. BLUEMOUND RD. P.O. BOX 13819 MILWAUKEE, WI 53213

Visit Hal Leonard Online at
www.halleonard.com

BIOGRAPHY

One of the most important bandleaders of the swing era, pianist William "Count" Basie, was born in New Jersey in 1904. Both of his parents were musicians. His father Harvie played the mellophone. It was his mother Lillian, a pianist, who first taught her son how to play. Basie also studied with Harlem stride pianists, most notably Fats Waller.

His first paying work was accompanying touring vaudeville performers. In 1927, the vaudeville troupe broke up while in Kansas City, leaving Basie stranded there. He found work playing for silent movies before joining Walter Page's Blue Devils in 1928. The following year he was lured away to play with Bennie Moten's band. As a member of the band, Basie played what would be a key role in the development of the Kansas City style of jazz. Upon Moten's untimely death in 1935, Basie put together a nine-piece ensemble made up of former members of the Blue Devils and the Moten band, called the Barons of Rhythm. Freddie Green, Jo Jones and Lester Young were all part of this group, which eventually gained residency at the Reno Club in Kansas City. Their performances were broadcast over radio, where an announcer dubbed the pianist "Count". This exposure led to contracts with a national booking agency and the Decca Record Company.

Expanding to a 13-piece band, the Count Basie Orchestra soon became one of the leading bands of the era, and its recording of "One O'Clock Jump" became a chart success in 1937. They spent the first part of the 1940s touring extensively, but after the U.S. entry into World War II and the subsequent recording ban, their travel became restricted. While on the West Coast, the band appeared in five films: *Hit Parade of 1943, Reveille with Beverly, Stage Door Canteen, Top Man* and *Crazy House*. The end of the decade saw a decline in the popularity of big bands, and Basie disbanded his band soon after, opting to lead smaller groups. By 1952 he was able to reform his big band because of increased opportunities for touring. This band would continue to tour and record extensively into the 1970s, garnering awards and acclaim along the way.

During his last decade, Basie recorded in a variety of small group settings, with sidemen such as Louis Bellson, Zoot Sims and Oscar Peterson. It is his piano work in these recordings that are represented in this transcription book.

Count Basie COLLECTION

After You've Gone

from *The Timekeepers – Count Basie Meets Oscar Peterson*
Words by Henry Creamer
Music by Turner Layton

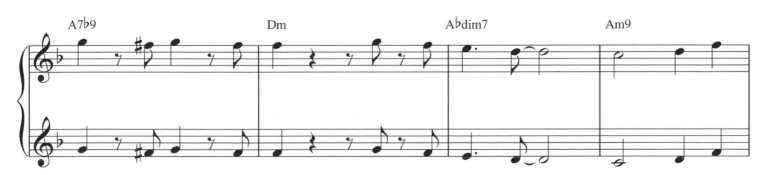

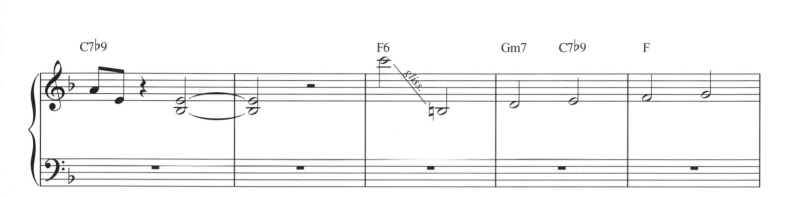

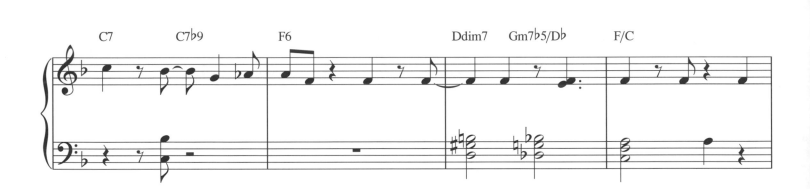

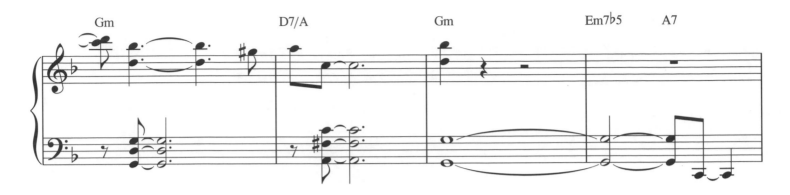

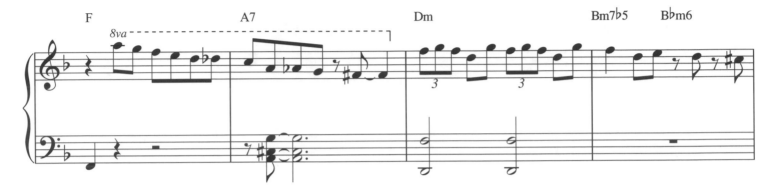

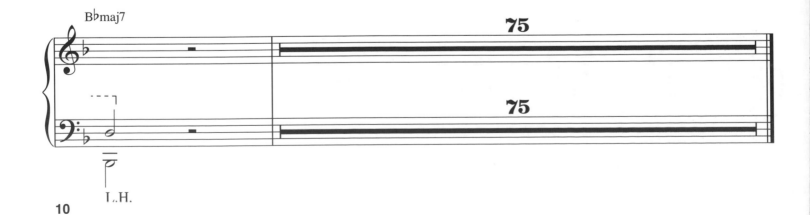

Exactly Like You

from *Satch and Josh*

Words by Dorothy Fields
Music by Jimmy McHugh

Moderate Swing ♩ = 133

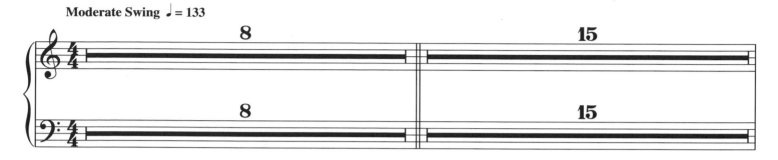

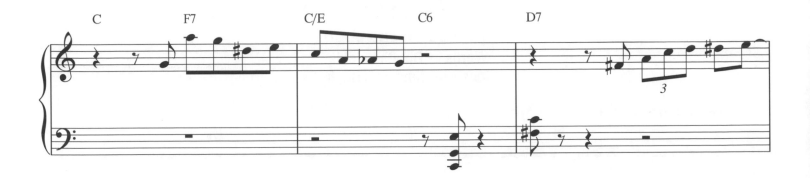

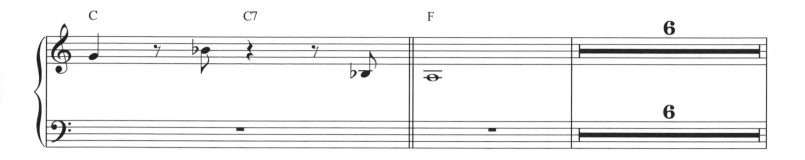

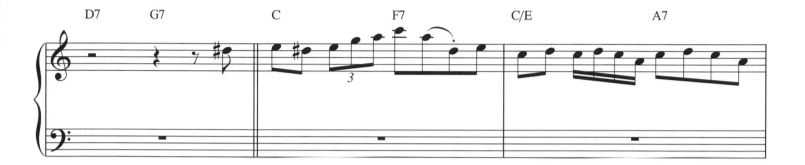

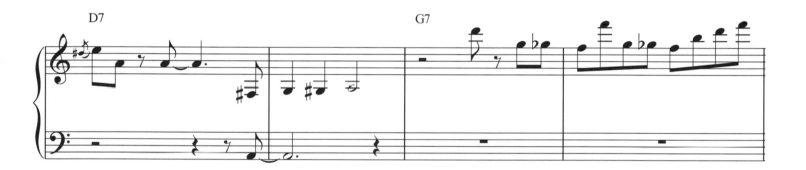

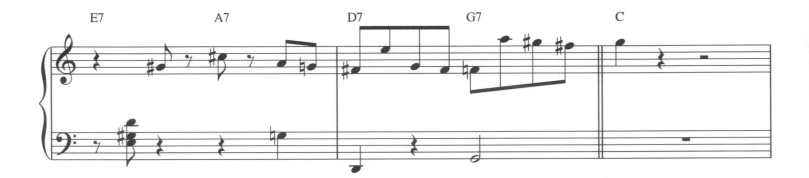

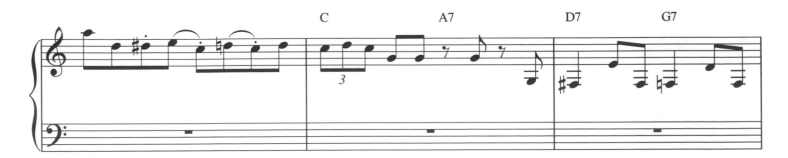

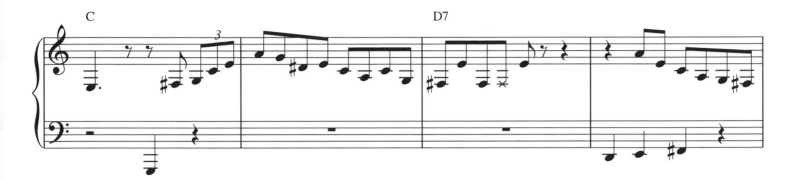

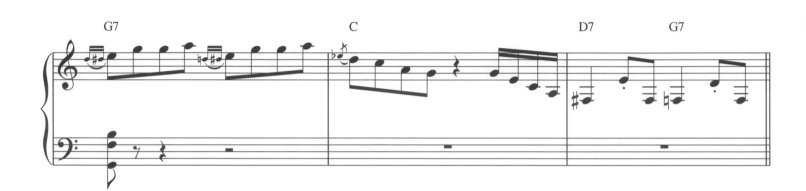

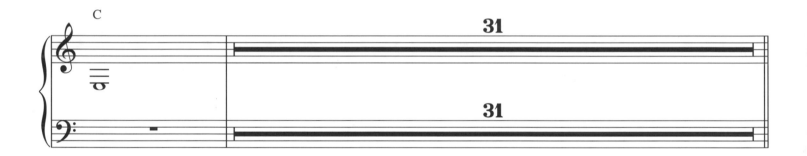

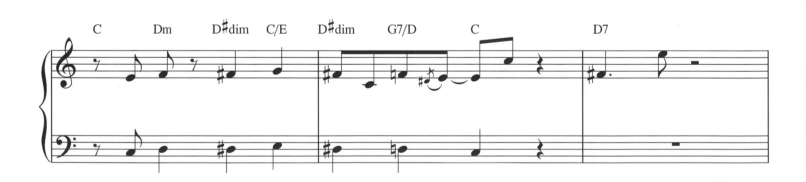

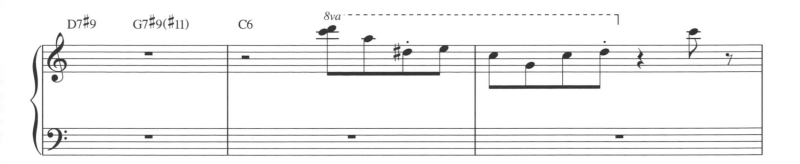

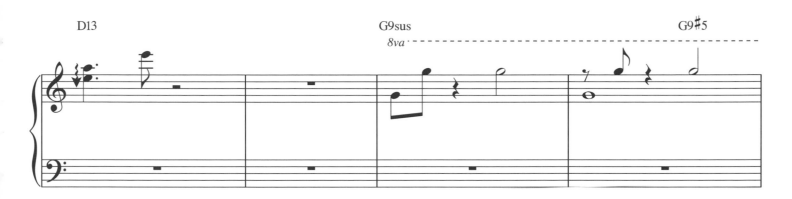

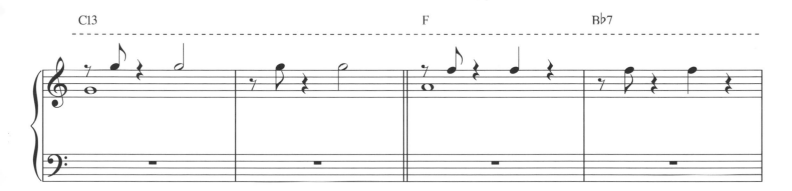

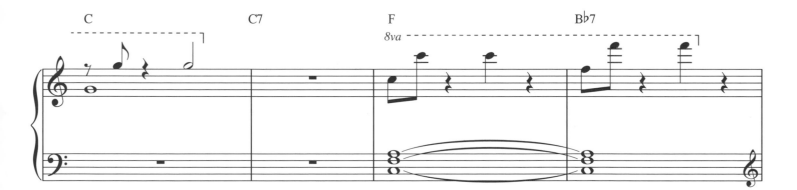

Honeysuckle Rose

from *Basie & Zoot*

Words by Andy Razaf
Music by Thomas "Fats" Waller

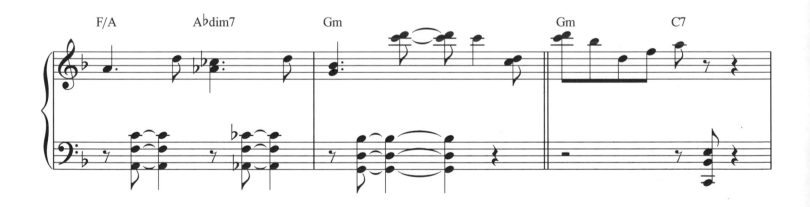

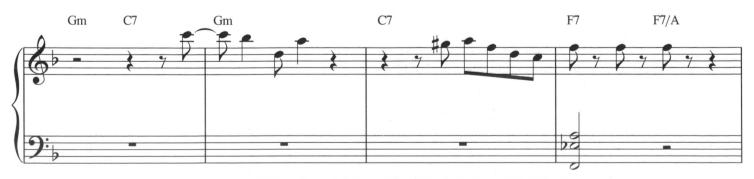

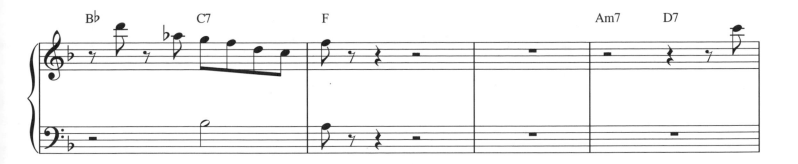

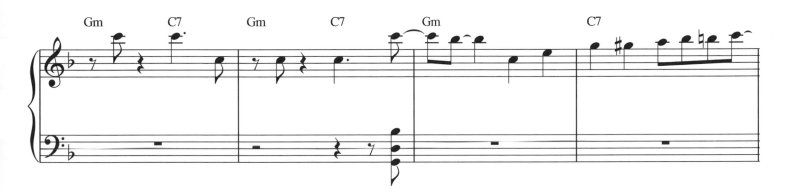

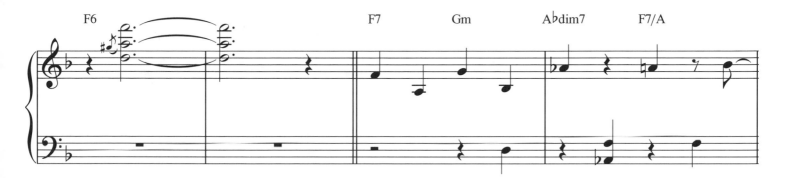

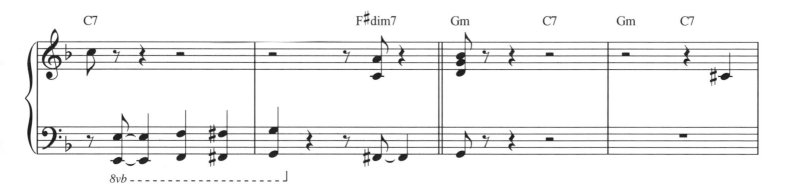

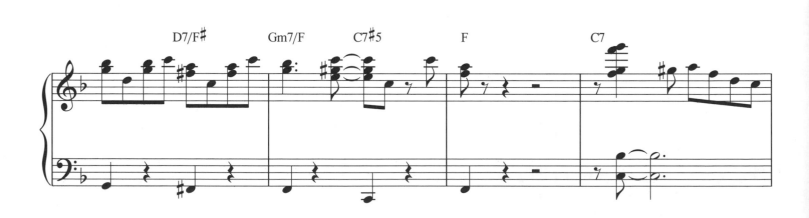

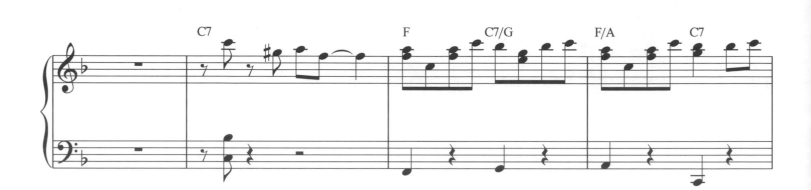

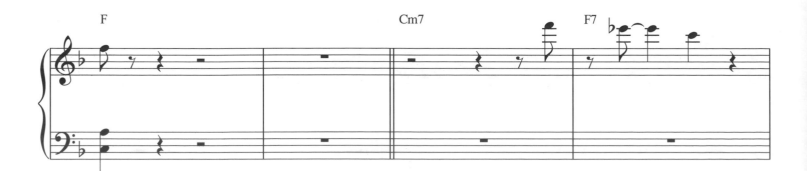

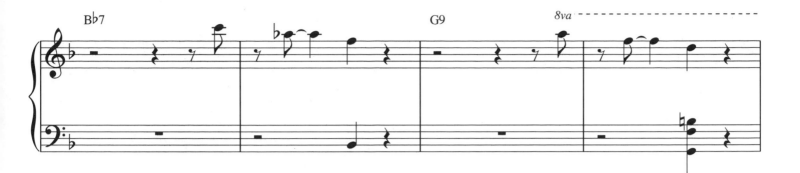

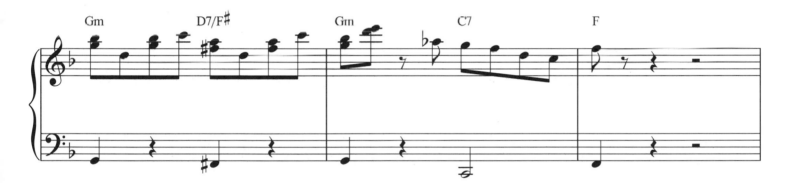

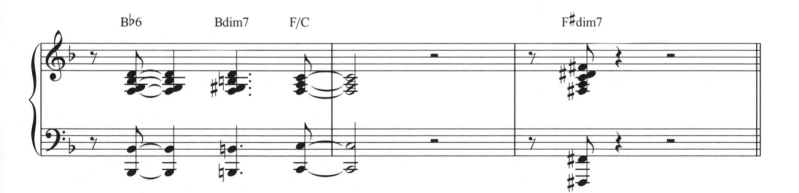

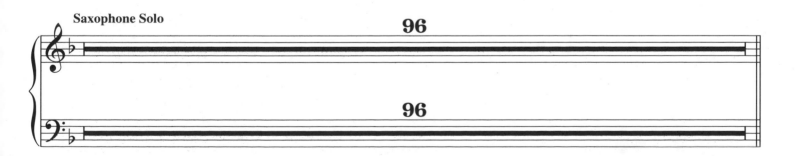

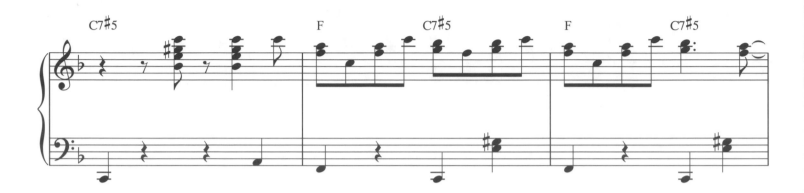

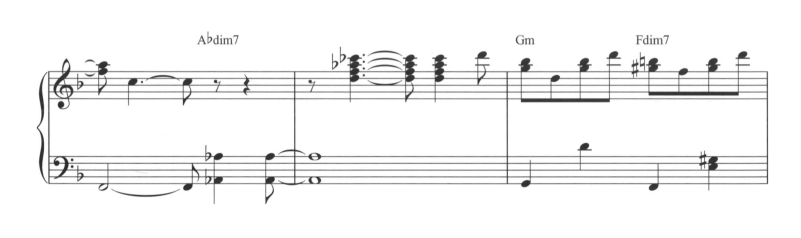

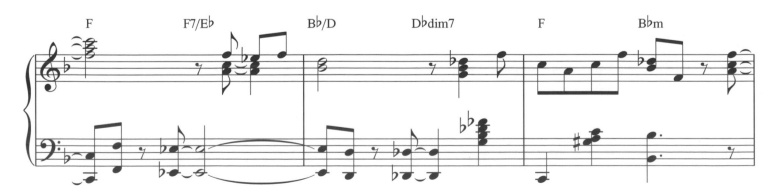

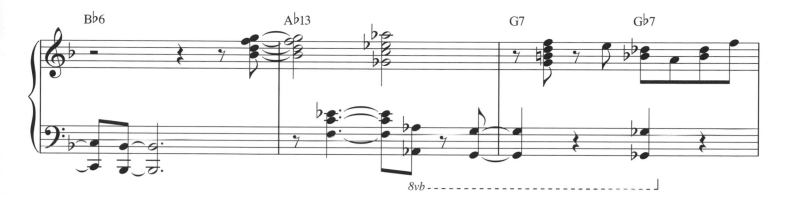

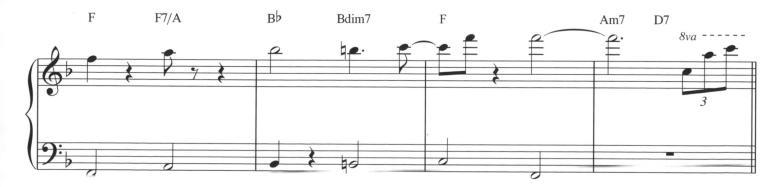

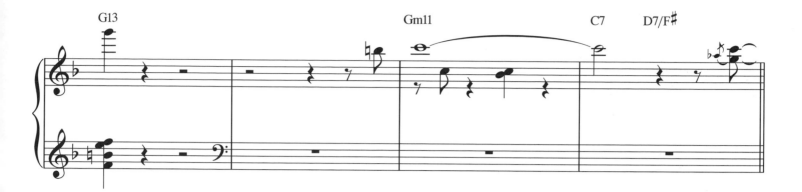

Trading Fours (Saxophone)

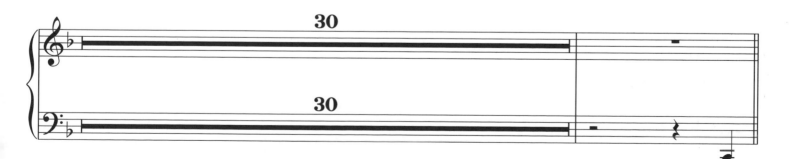

Ad lib. (With Saxophone)

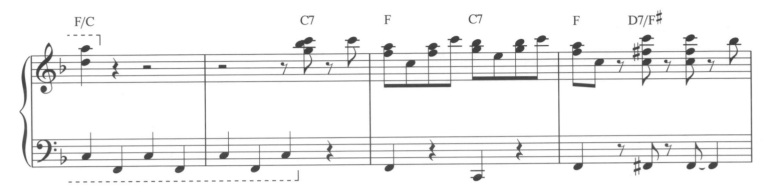

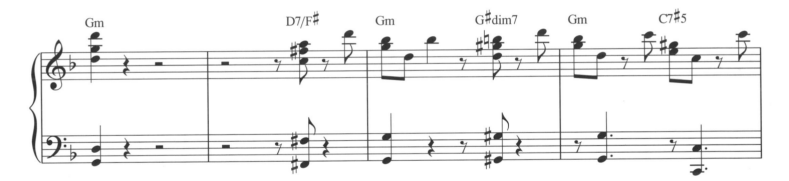

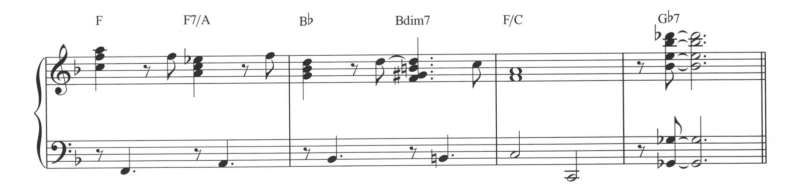

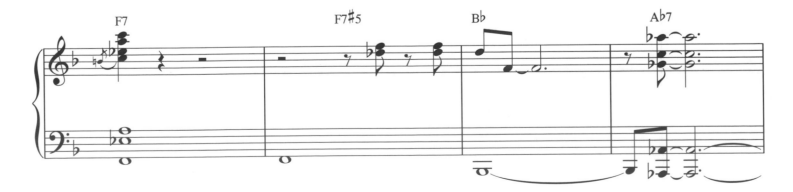

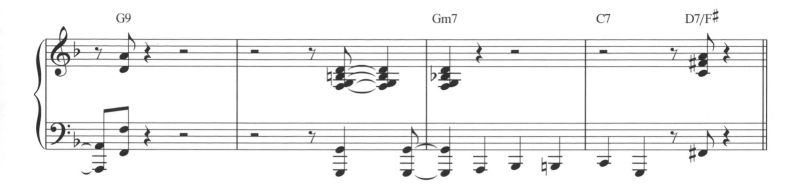

("Comp"-Sax Solo)

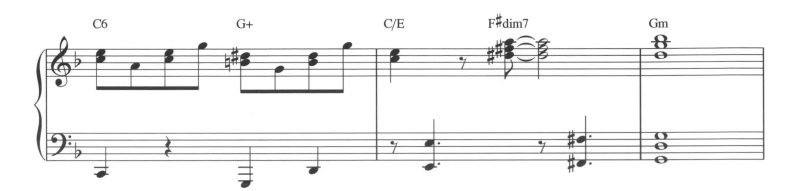

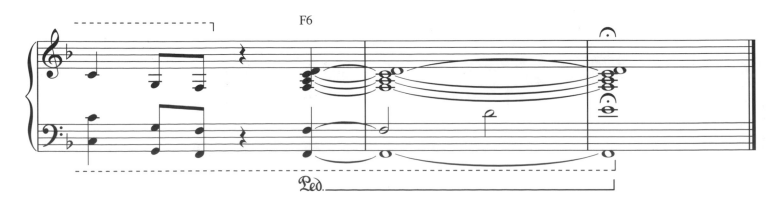

I'll Always Be in Love with You

from *For the First Time*

Words and Music by Bud Green,
Herman Ruby and Sam H. Stept

Medium Swing ♩ = 138

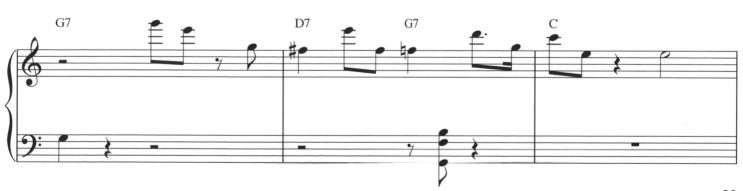

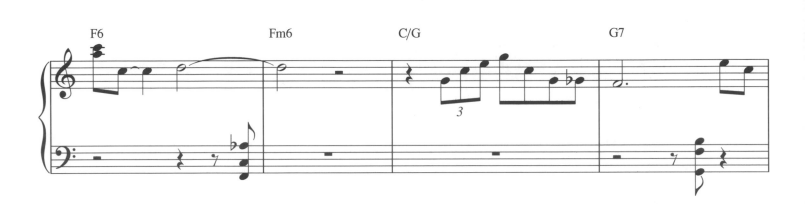

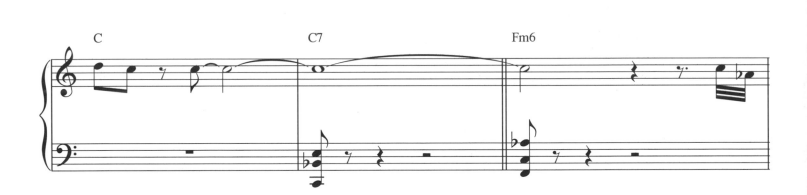

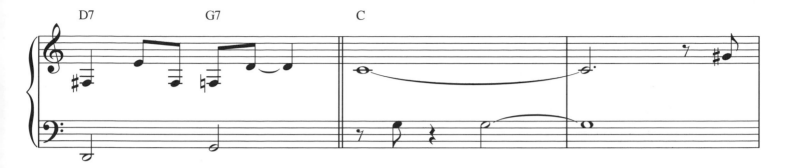

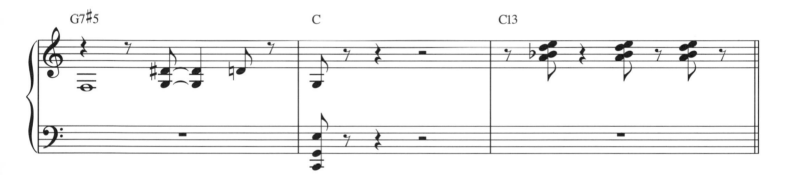

Bass Solo

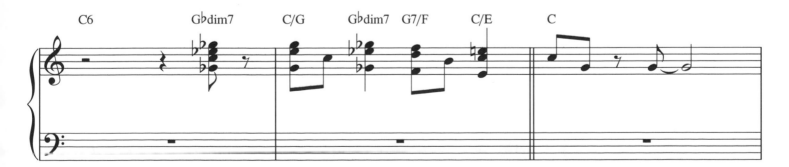

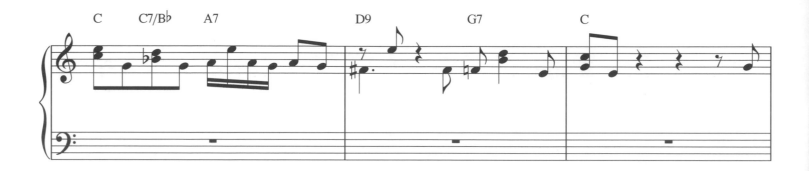

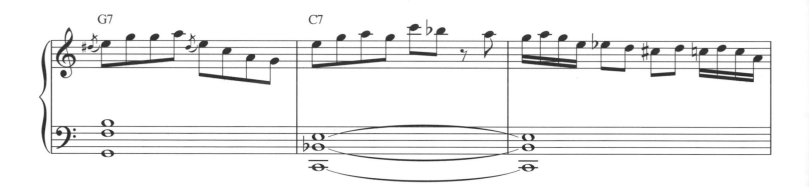

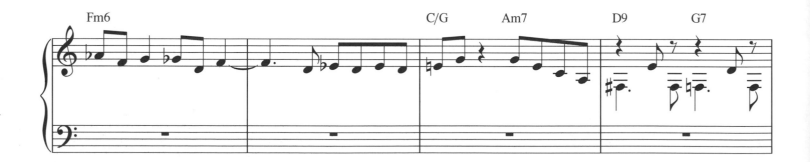

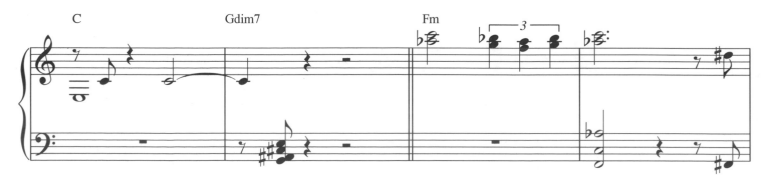

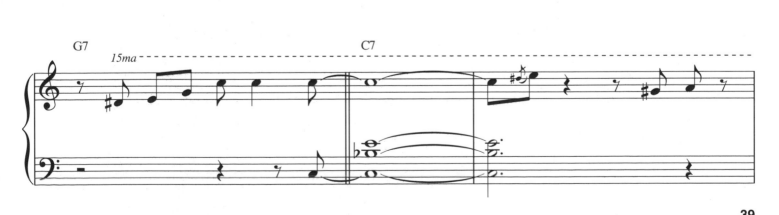

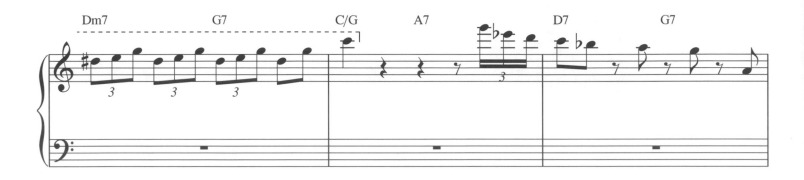

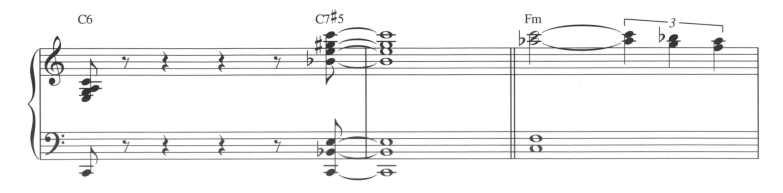

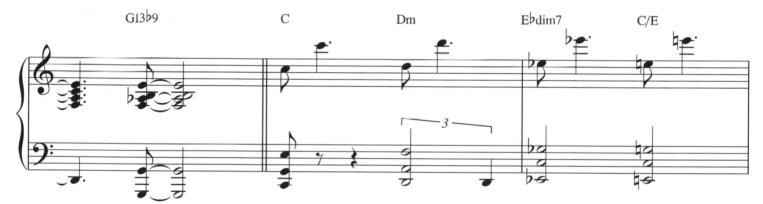

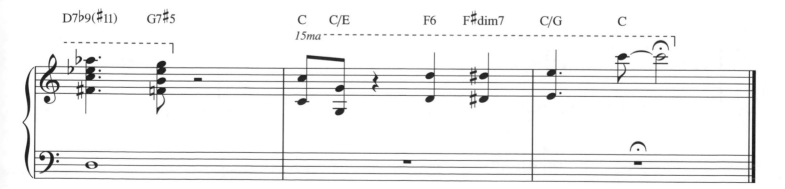

Indiana

(Back Home Again in Indiana)
from *The Timekeepers – Count Basie Meets Oscar Peterson*
Words by Ballard MacDonald
Music by James F. Hanley

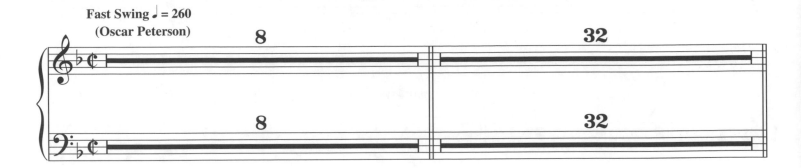

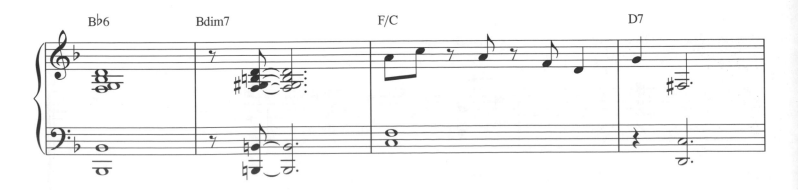

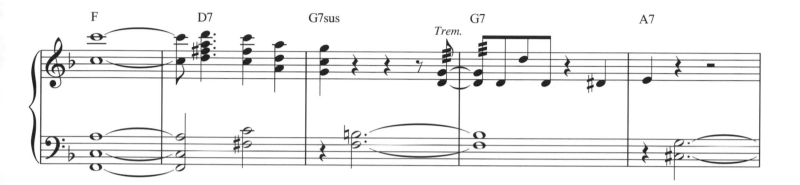

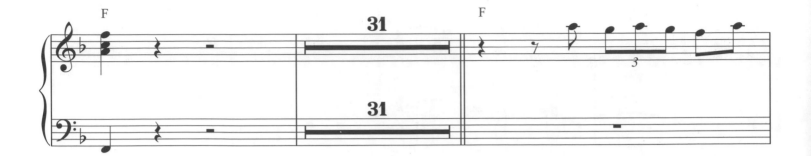

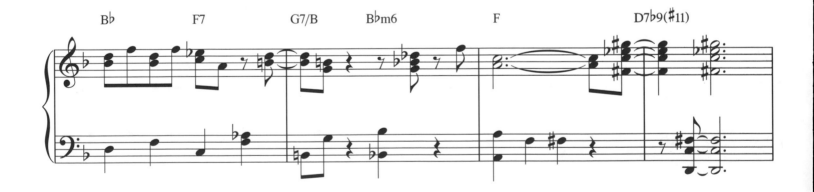

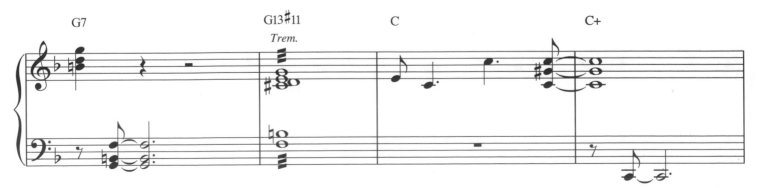

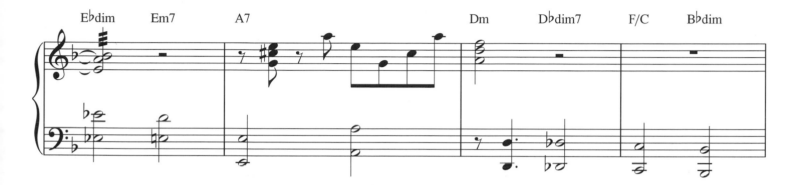

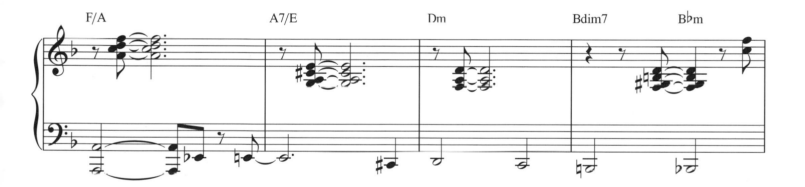

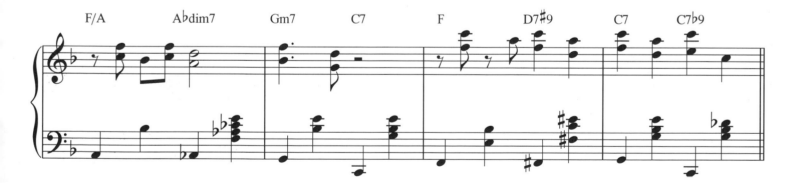

It's Only a Paper Moon

from *Basie & Zoot*

Lyric by Billy Rose and E.Y. Harburg
Music by Harold Arlen

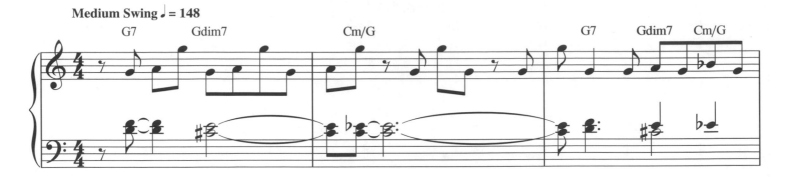

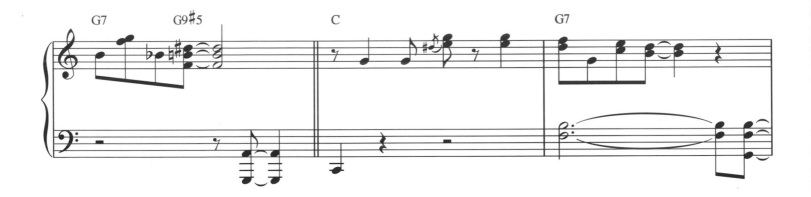

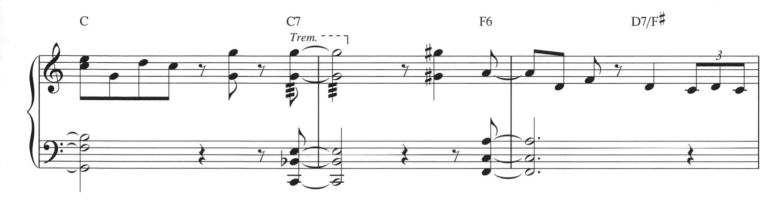

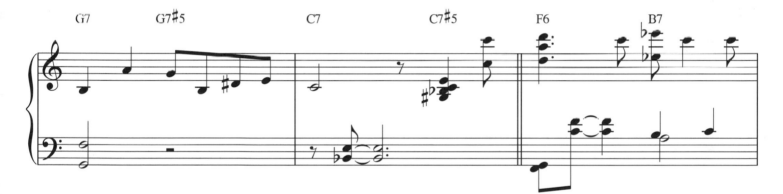

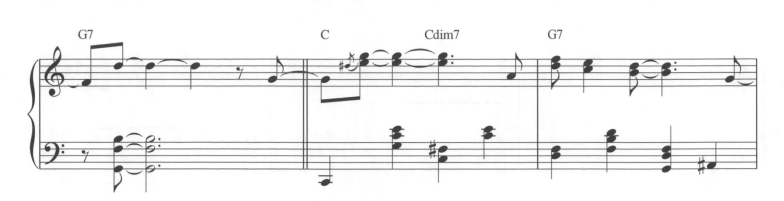

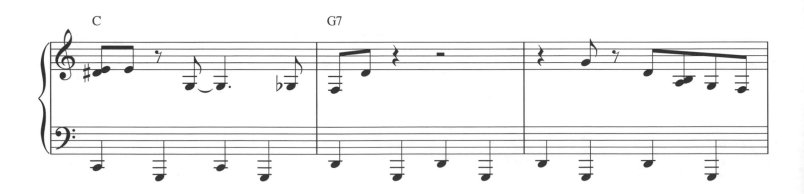

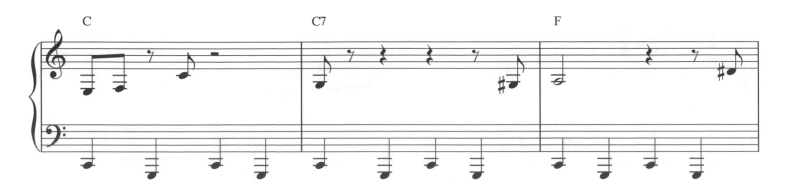

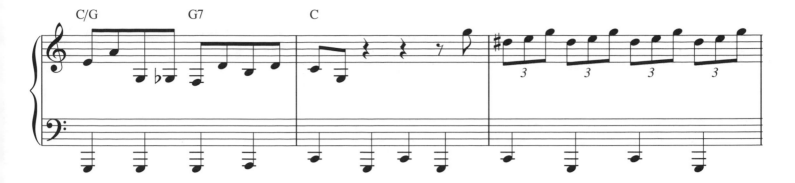

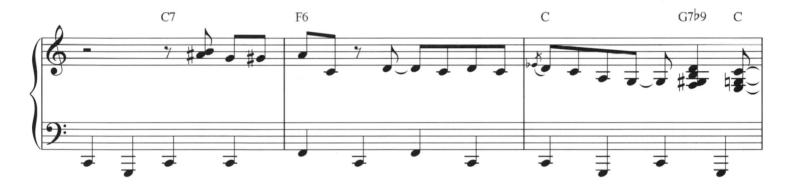

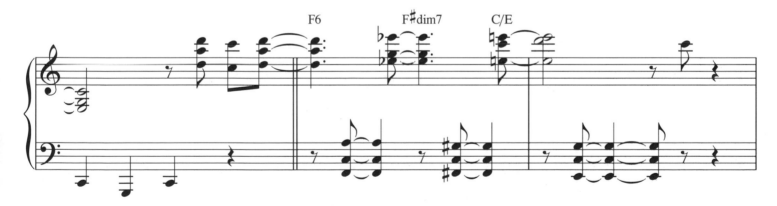

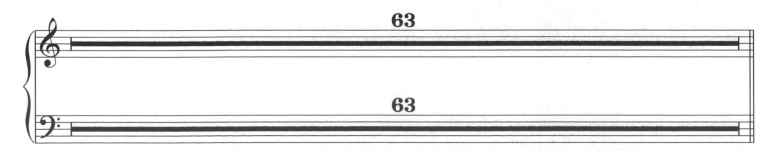

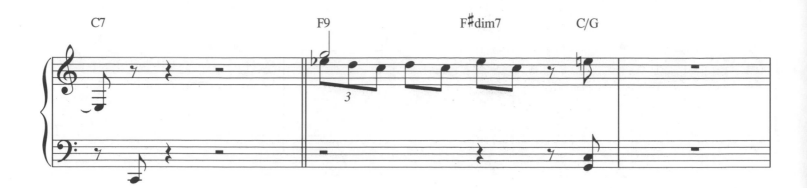

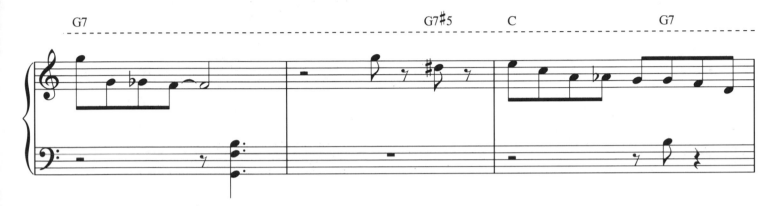

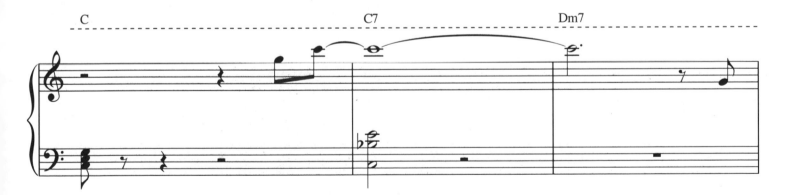

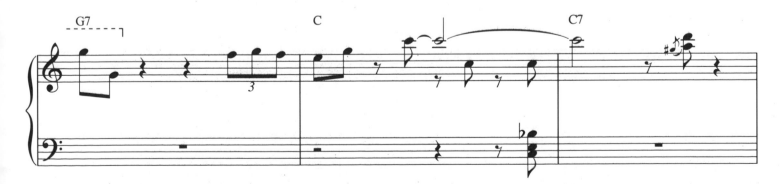

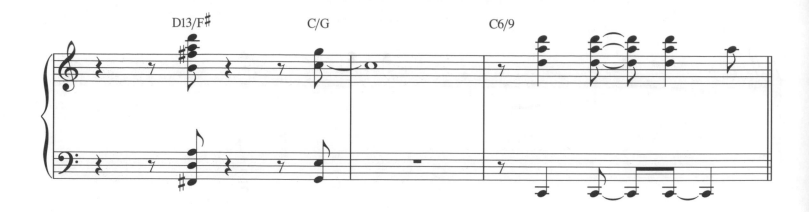

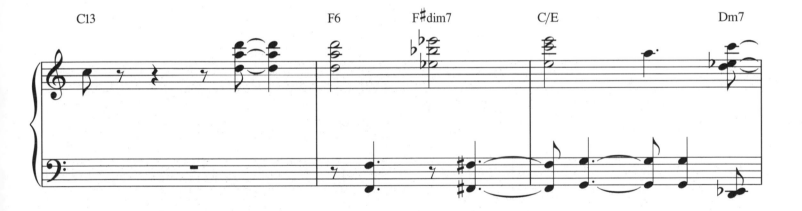

Jumpin' at the Woodside

from *Satch and Josh*
Music by Count Basie

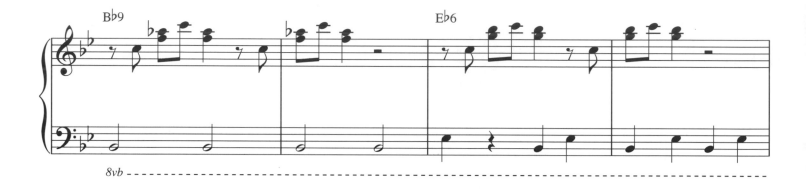

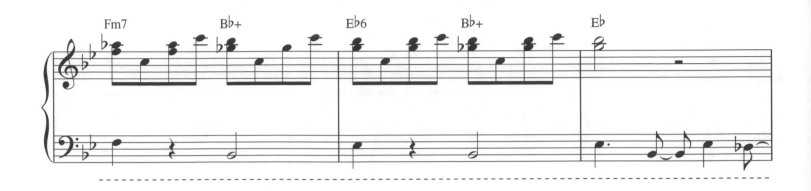

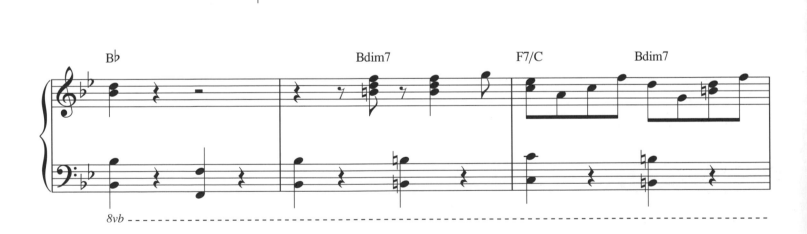

(Trading fours)

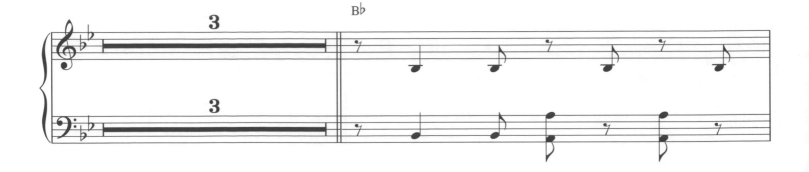

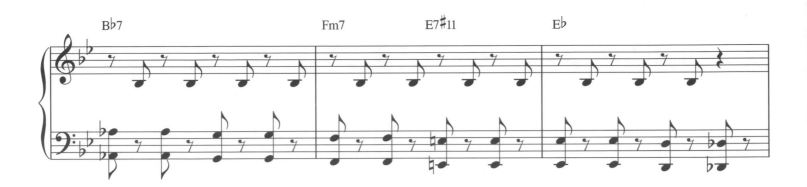

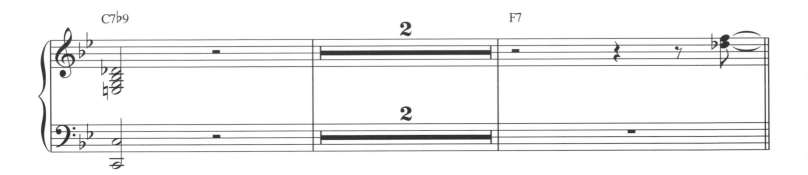

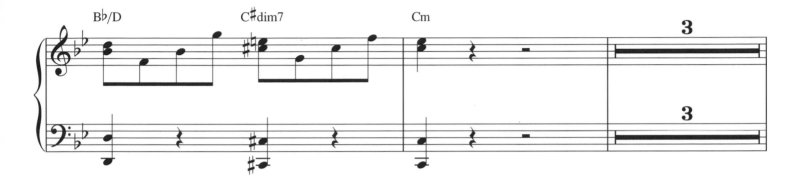

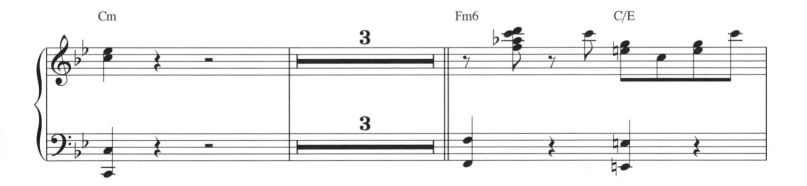

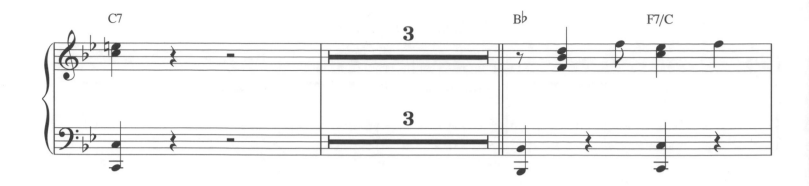

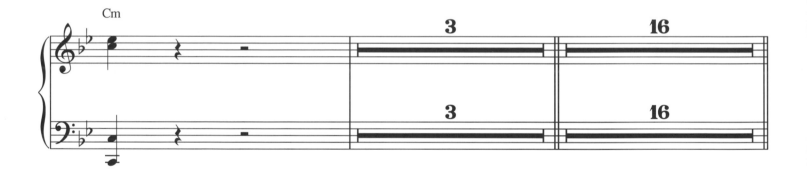

Mean to Me
from *Basie & Zoot*
Lyric and Music by Fred E. Ahlert
and Roy Turk

Medium Swing ♩ = 122

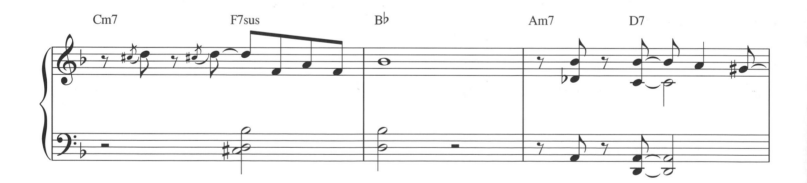

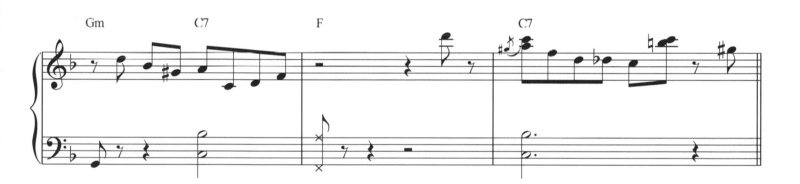

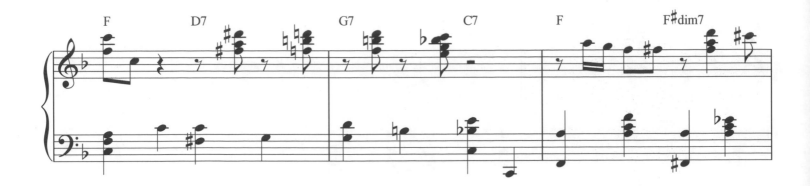

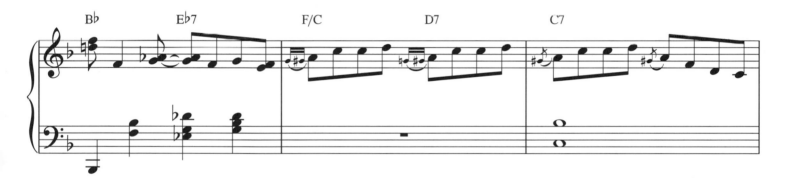

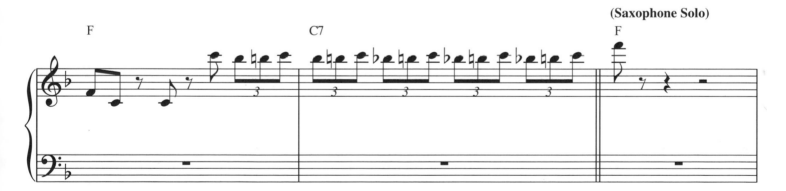

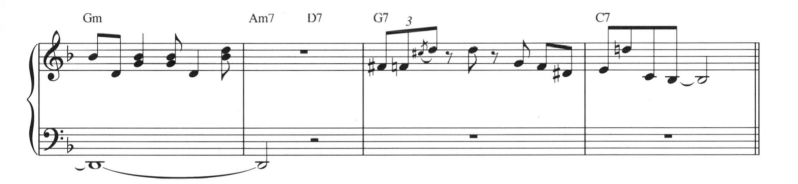

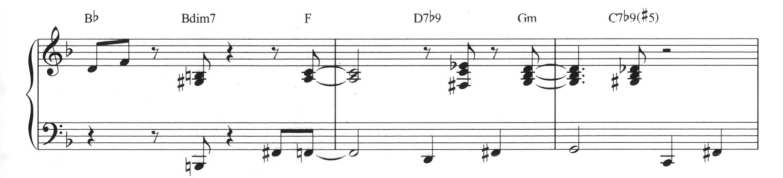

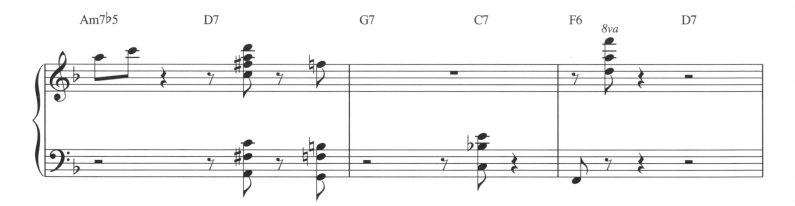

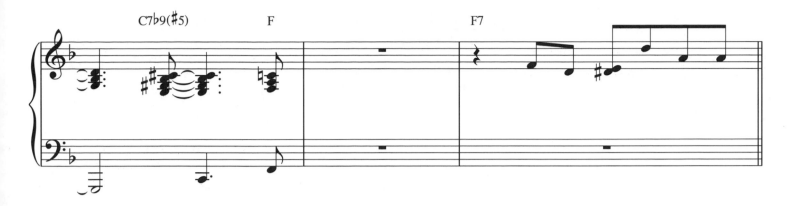

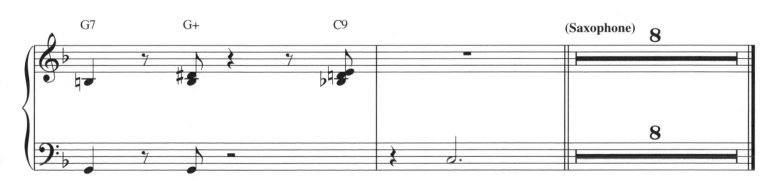

Memories of You

from *Kansas City 5*

Lyric by Andy Razaf
Music by Eubie Blake

Moderate Ballad ♩ = 108

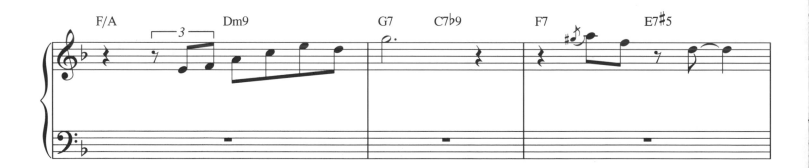

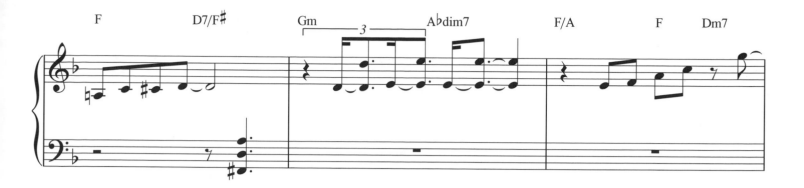

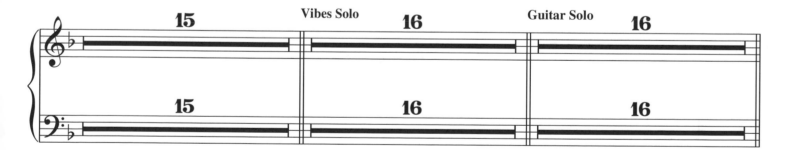

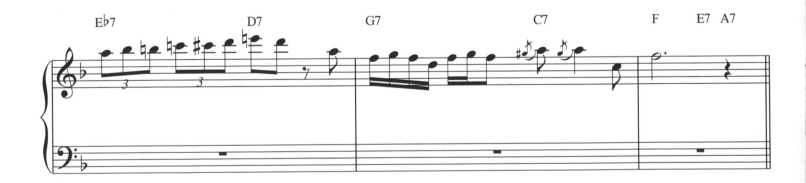

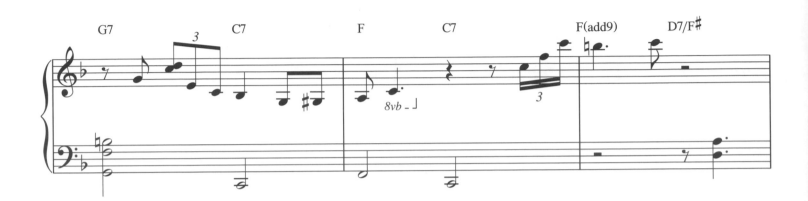

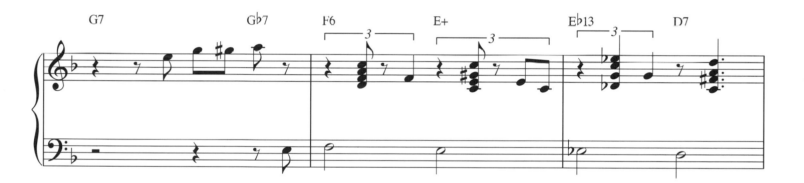

9:20 Special

from *Night Rider*
By Earl Warren
and Buster Harding

Moderate Swing ♩ = 186

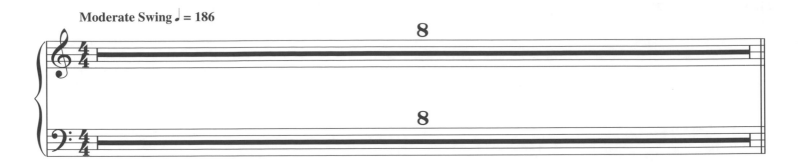

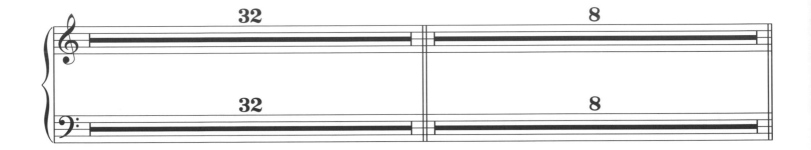

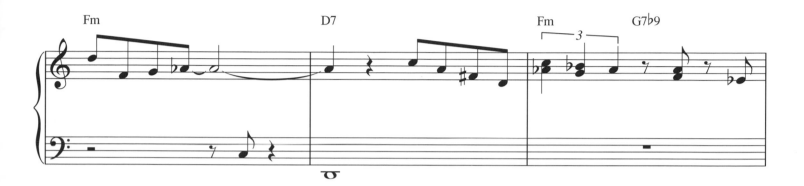

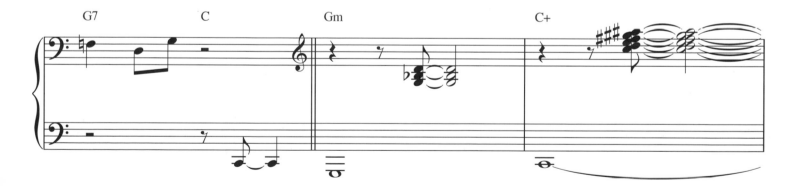

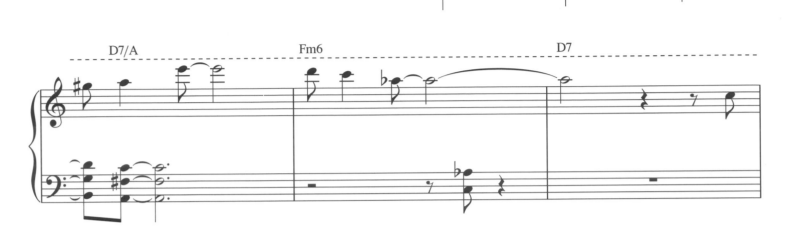

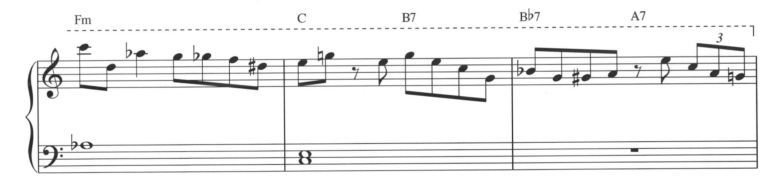

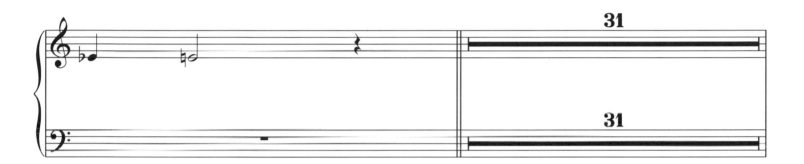

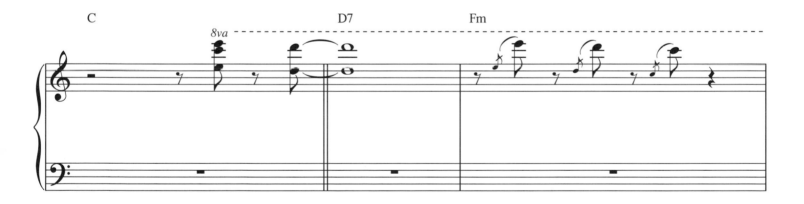

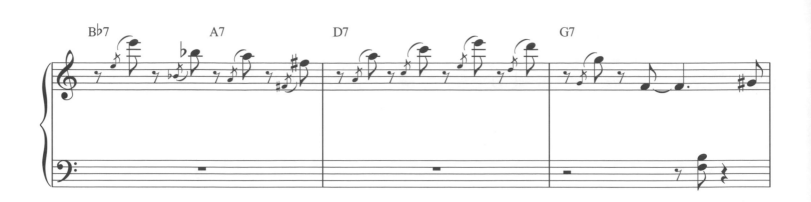

On the Sunny Side of the Street

from *For the Second Time*

Lyric by Dorothy Fields
Music by Jimmy McHugh

Moderate Swing ♩ = 110

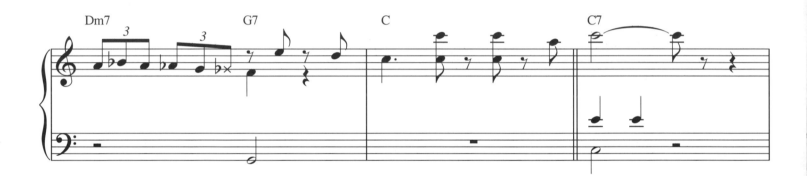

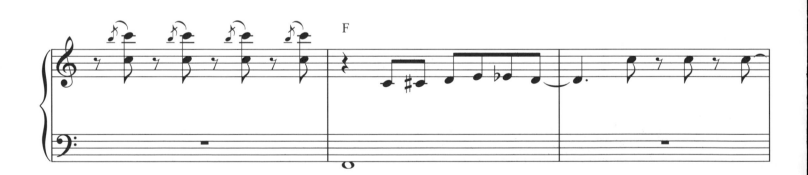

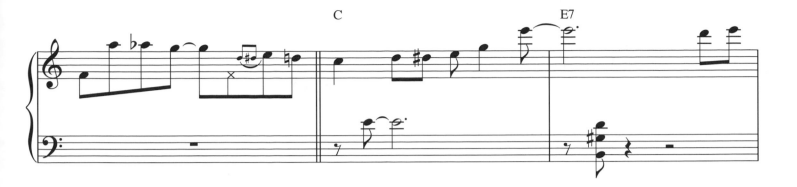

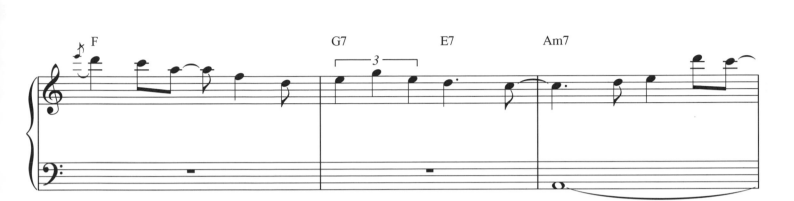

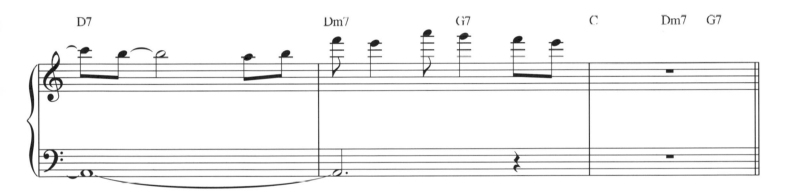

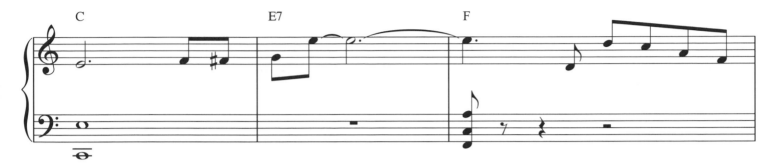

Bass Solo

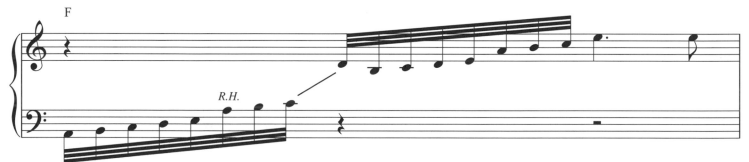

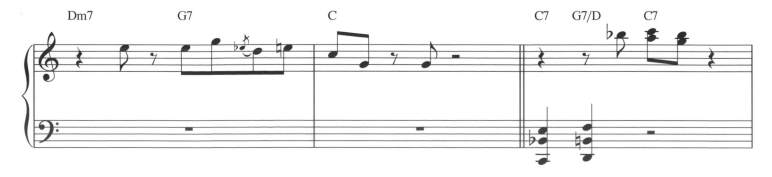

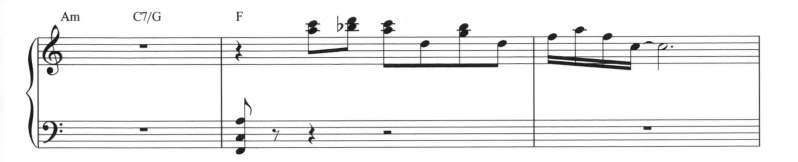

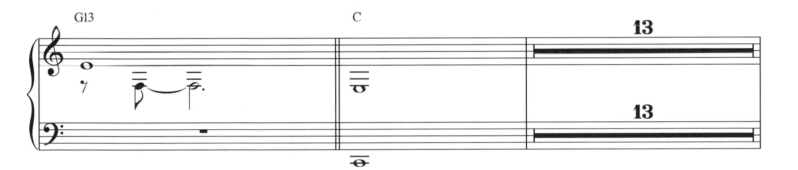

One O'Clock Jump

from *Kansas City 5*

By Count Basie

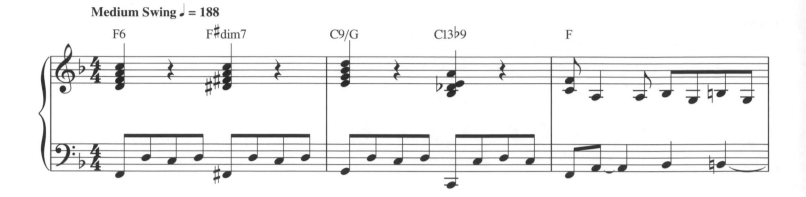

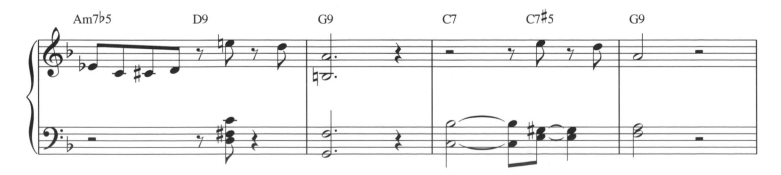

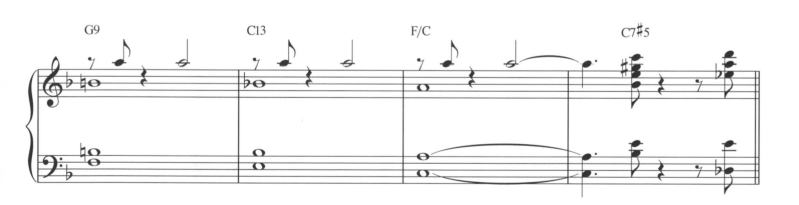

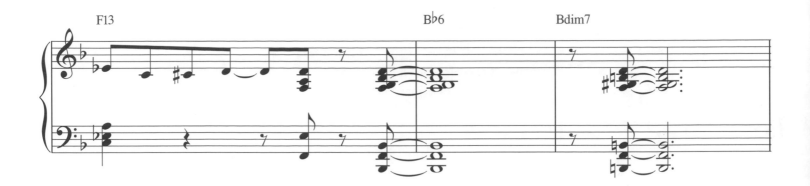

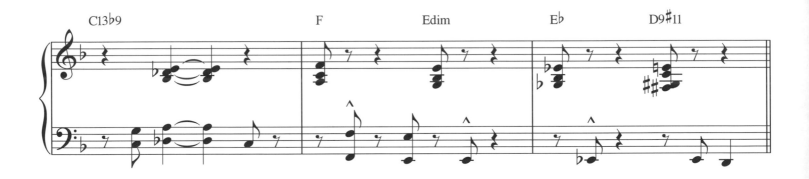

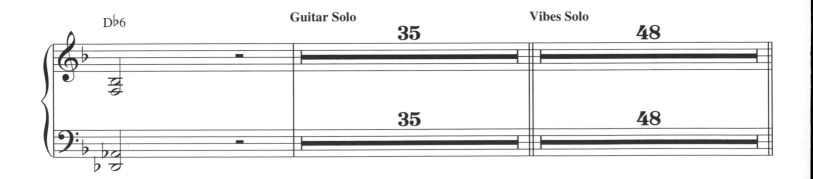

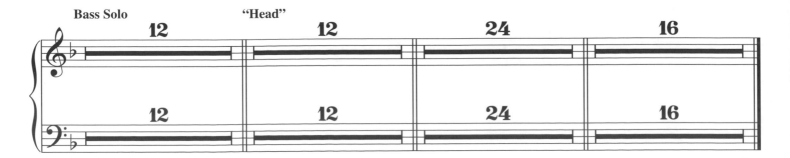

Poor Butterfly

from *Yessir, That's My Baby*

Words by John L. Golden
Music by Raymond Hubbell

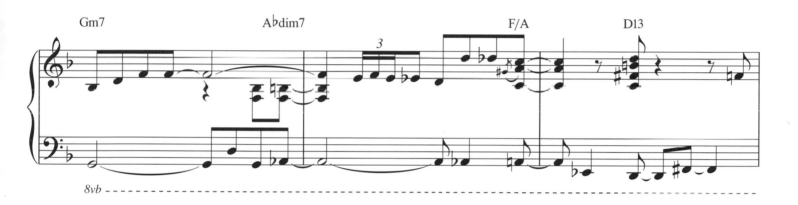

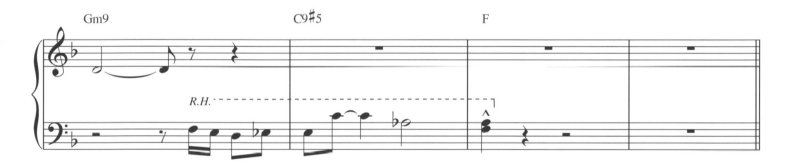

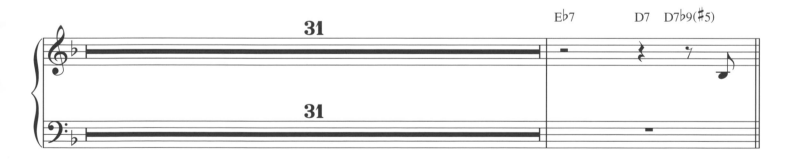

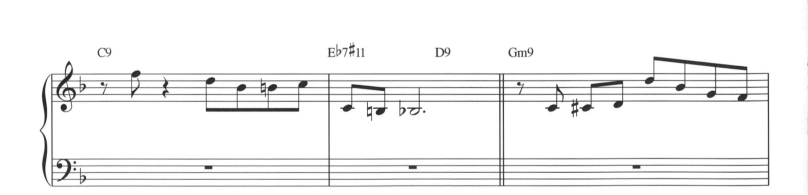

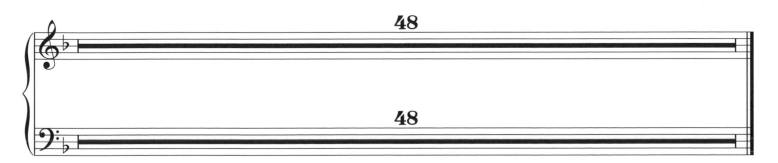

Roots

from *Satch and Josh...Again*

Words and Music by Count Basie
and Oscar Peterson

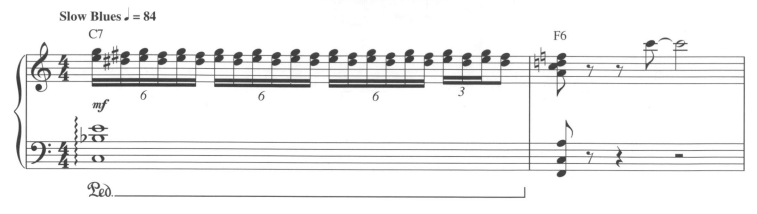

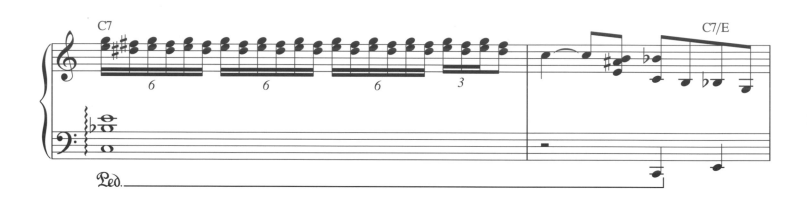

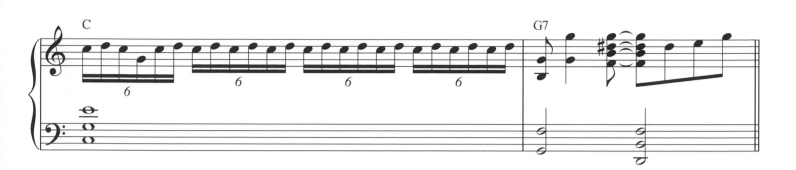

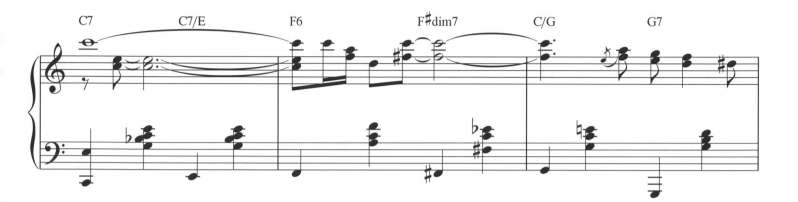

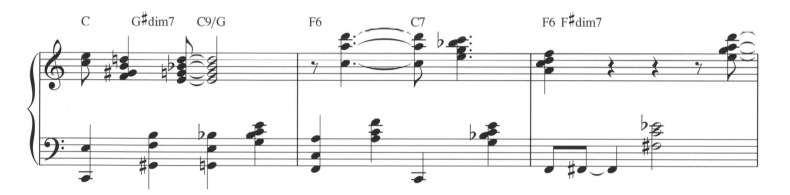

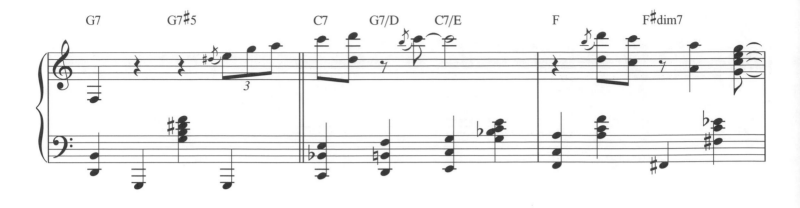

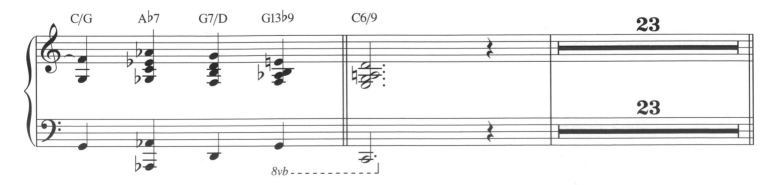

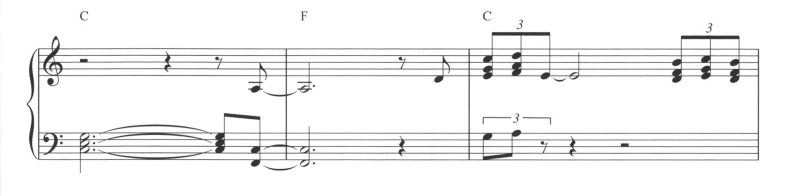

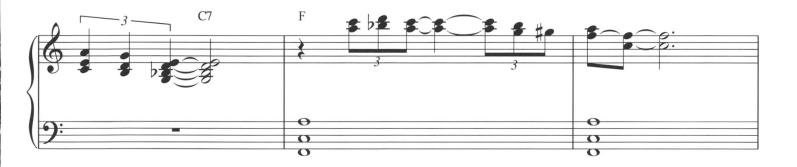

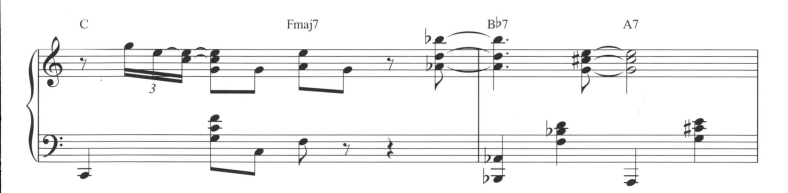

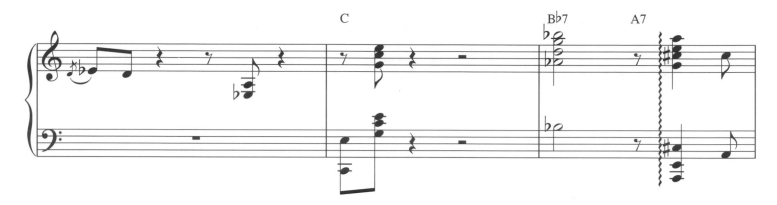

(Duet ad lib. between Basie and Peterson)

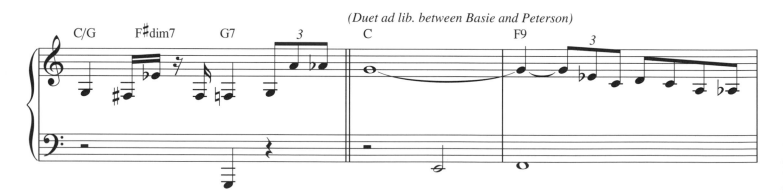

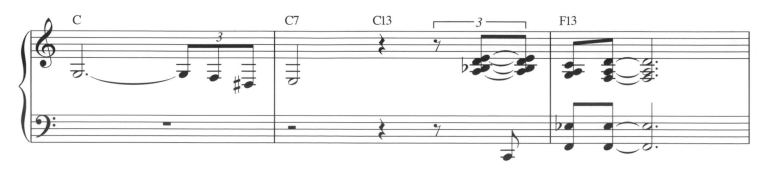

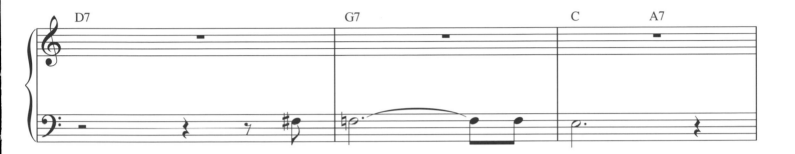

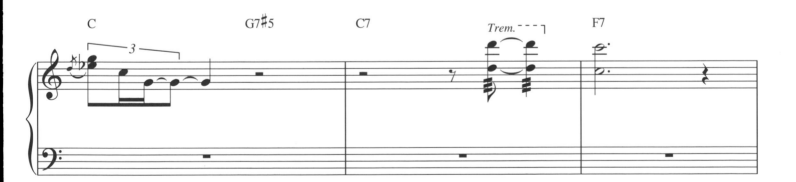

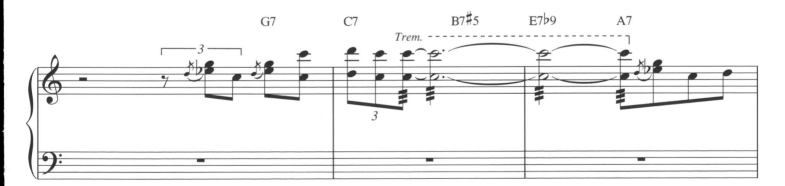

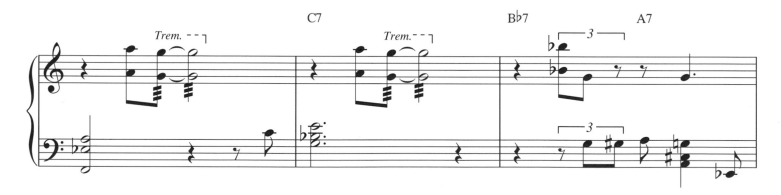

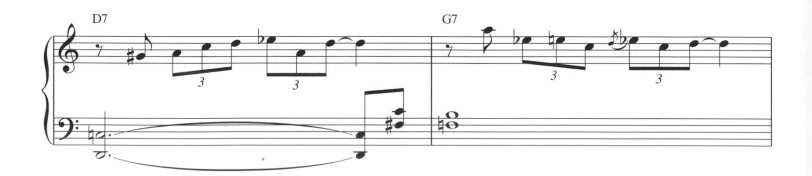

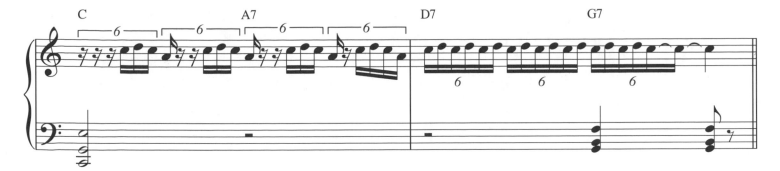

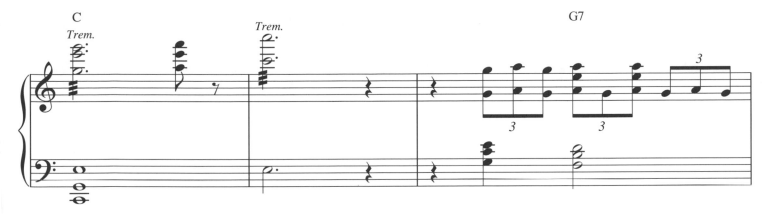

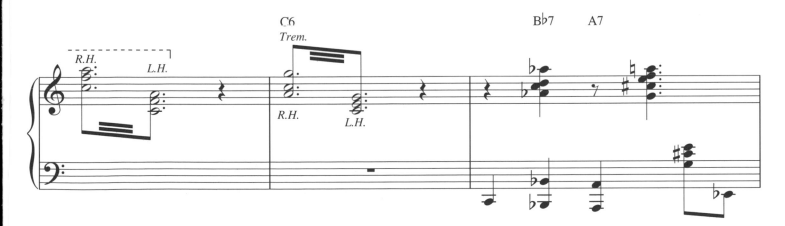

ARTIST TRANSCRIPTIONS

Artist Transcriptions are authentic, note-for-note transcriptions of the hottest artists in jazz, pop, and rock today. These outstanding, accurate arrangements are in an easy-to-read format which includes all essential lines. Artist Transcriptions can be used to perform, sequence or reference.

GUITAR & BASS

The Guitar Style of George Benson
00660113 ....$14.95

The Guitar Book of Pierre Bensusan
00699072 ....$19.95

Ron Carter – Acoustic Bass
00672331 ....$16.95

Stanley Clarke Collection
00672307 ....$19.95

Al Di Meola – Cielo E Terra
00604041 ....$14.95

Al Di Meola – Friday Night in San Francisco
00660115 ....$14.95

Al Di Meola – Music, Words, Pictures
00604043 ....$14.95

Kevin Eubanks Guitar Collection
00672319 ....$19.95

The Jazz Style of Tal Farlow
00673245 ....$19.95

Bela Fleck and the Flecktones
00672359 Melody/Lyrics/Chords $18.95

David Friesen – Years Through Time
00673253 ....$14.95

Best of Frank Gambale
00672336 ....$22.95

Jim Hall – Jazz Guitar Environments
00699389 Book/CD $19.95

Jim Hall – Exploring Jazz Guitar
00699306 ....$17.95

Allan Holdsworth –
Reaching for the Uncommon Chord
00604049 ....$14.95

Leo Kottke – Eight Songs
00699215 ....$14.95

Wes Montgomery – Guitar Transcriptions
00675536 ....$17.95

Joe Pass Collection
00672353 ....$18.95

John Patitucci
00673216 ....$14.95

Django Reinhardt Anthology
00027083 ....$14.95

The Genius of Django Reinhardt
00026711 ....$10.95

Django Reinhardt – A Treasury of Songs
00026715 ....$12.95

Johnny Smith Guitar Solos
00672374 ....$16.95

Mike Stern Guitar Book
00673224 ....$16.95

Mark Whitfield
00672320 ....$19.95

Jack Wilkins – Windows
00673249 ....$14.95

Gary Willis Collection
00672337 ....$19.95

SAXOPHONE

Julian "Cannonball" Adderly Collection
00673244 ....$19.95

Michael Brecker
00673237 ....$19.95

Michael Brecker Collection
00672429 ....$19.95

The Brecker Brothers...
And All Their Jazz
00672351 ....$19.95

Best of the Brecker Brothers
00672447 ....$19.95

Benny Carter Plays Standards
00672315 ....$22.95

Benny Carter Collection
00672314 ....$22.95

James Carter Collection
00672394 ....$19.95

John Coltrane – Giant Steps
00672349 ....$19.95

John Coltrane – A Love Supreme
00672494 ....$12.95

John Coltrane Plays "Coltrane Changes"
00672493 ....$19.95

Coltrane Plays Standards
00672453 ....$19.95

John Coltrane Solos
00673233 ....$22.95

Paul Desmond Collection
00672328 ....$19.95

Paul Desmond – Standard Time
00672454 ....$19.95

Stan Getz
00699375 ....$18.95

Stan Getz – Bossa Novas
00672377 ....$19.95

Stan Getz – Standards
00672375 ....$17.95

The Coleman Hawkins Collection
00672523 ....$19.95

Joe Henderson – Selections from
"Lush Life" & "So Near So Far"
00673252 ....$19.95

Best of Joe Henderson
00672330 ....$22.95

Best of Kenny G
00673239 ....$19.95

Kenny G – Breathless
00673229 ....$19.95

Kenny G – Classics in the Key of G
00672462 ....$19.95

Kenny G – Faith: A Holiday Album
00672485 ....$14.95

Kenny G – The Moment
00672373 ....$19.95

Kenny G – Paradise
00672516 ....$14.95

Joe Lovano Collection
00672326 ....$19.95

James Moody Collection – Sax and Flute
00672372 ....$19.95

The Frank Morgan Collection
00672416 ....$19.95

The Art Pepper Collection
00672301 ....$19.95

Sonny Rollins Collection
00672444 ....$19.95

David Sanborn Collection
00675000 ....$16.95

The Lew Tabackin Collection
00672455 ....$19.95

Stanley Turrentine Collection
00672334 ....$19.95

Ernie Watts Saxophone Collection
00673256 ....$18.95

PIANO & KEYBOARD

Monty Alexander Collection
00672338 ....$19.95

Monty Alexander Plays Standards
00672487 ....$19.95

Kenny Barron Collection
00672318 ....$22.95

The Count Basie Collection
00672520 ....$19.95

Warren Bernhardt Collection
00672364 ....$19.95

Cyrus Chesnut Collection
00672439 ....$19.95

Billy Childs Collection
00673242 ....$19.95

Chick Corea – Elektric Band
00603126 ....$15.95

Chick Corea – Paint the World
00672300 ....$12.95

Bill Evans Collection
00672365 ....$19.95

Bill Evans – Piano Interpretations
00672425 ....$19.95

The Bill Evans Trio
00672510 Volume 1: 1959-1961 ......$24.95
00672511 Volume 2: 1962-1965 ......$24.95
00672512 Volume 3: 1968-1974 ......$24.95
00672513 Volume 4: 1979-1980 ......$24.95

The Benny Goodman Collection
00672492 ....$16.95

Benny Green Collection
00672329 ....$19.95

Vince Guaraldi Jazz Transcriptions
00672486 ....$19.95

Herbie Hancock Collection
00672419 ....$19.95

Gene Harris Collection
00672446 ....$19.95

Hampton Hawes
00672438 ....$19.95

Ahmad Jamal Collection
00672322 ....$22.95

Brad Mehldau Collection
00672476 ....$19.95

Thelonious Monk Plays Jazz Standards – Volume 1
00672390 ....$19.95

Thelonious Monk Plays Jazz Standards – Volume 2
00672391 ....$19.95

Thelonious Monk – Intermediate Piano Solos
00672392 ....$14.95

Jelly Roll Morton – The Piano Rolls
00672433 ....$12.95

Michel Petrucciani
00673226 ....$17.95

Bud Powell Classics
00672371 ....$19.95

Bud Powell Collection
00672376 ....$19.95

André Previn Collection
00672437 ....$19.95

Gonzalo Rubalcaba Collection
00672507 ....$19.95

Horace Silver Collection
00672303 ....$19.95

Art Tatum Collection
00672316 ....$22.95

Art Tatum Solo Book
00672355 ....$19.95

Billy Taylor Collection
00672357 ....$24.95

McCoy Tyner
00673215 ....$16.95

Cedar Walton Collection
00672321 ....$19.95

The Teddy Wilson Collection
00672434 ....$19.95

CLARINET

Buddy De Franco Collection
00672423 ....$19.95

TROMBONE

J.J. Johnson Collection
00672332 ....$19.95

TRUMPET

The Chet Baker Collection
00672435 ....$19.95

Randy Brecker
00673234 ....$17.95

The Brecker Brothers...And All Their Jazz
00672351 ....$19.95

Best of the Brecker Brothers
00672447 ....$19.95

Miles Davis – Originals Volume 1
00672448 ....$19.95

Miles Davis – Originals Volume 2
00672451 ....$19.95

Miles Davis – Standards Vol. 1
00672450 ....$19.95

Miles Davis – Standards Vol. 2
00672449 ....$19.95

The Dizzy Gillespie Collection
00672479 ....$19.95

Freddie Hubbard
00673214 ....$14.95

Tom Harrell Jazz Trumpet
00672382 ....$19.95

The Chuck Mangione Collection
00672506 ....$19.95

FLUTE

Eric Dolphy Collection
00672379 ....$19.95

James Newton – Improvising Flute
00660108 ....$14.95

The Lew Tabackin Collection
00672455 ....$19.95

For More Information, See Your Local Music Dealer,
Or Write To:

HAL•LEONARD® CORPORATION
7777 W. Bluemound Rd. P.O. Box 13819 Milwaukee, WI 53213

Prices and availability subject to change without notice.
Some products may not be available outside the U.S.A.

Visit our web site for a complete listing of our titles with songlists.
www.halleonard.com

0104